GO ON, GIRL!

written by

Candace Petty Smith

illustrated by

Hatice Bayramoglu

DEDICATION

To my girls K.S. and C.S., you will always be MORE than enough.

To any girl who has ever been told that you were *not* good enough,

hold your head high and show them just how good you are!

INSCRIPTION

_____,

YOU ARE SMART.
YOU ARE BEAUTIFUL.
YOU ARE ENOUGH.

Love,

_____

They say girls are not smart enough

but I have the best grades in my class.

They say girls are not thin enough but I can still walk the runway with all this sass.

They say girls are not pretty enough but real beauty lies on the inside of you.

They say girls are not fast enough but all of these medals show that that's not true.

They say girls can't play good enough

but I bet I can shoot better than you.

I can swish 3's, shoot free throws and

dribble circles around you, too!

They say our hair is not straight enough but my hair does not define my personality. It's my confidence, my character, my spirit, my laughter. It's everything that makes me--ME.

They say girls are not strong enough but I wear many hats as you can see. It's gonna take more than mean words or dirty looks to discourage or break me.

We're young but we've all had enough of being told what we can and cannot do.

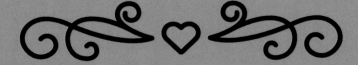

The only thing a girl hasn't done, just yet, is become President.

One day, we'll do that, too!

Never give up on your hopes and dreams because someone tells you no. Just give them a smile, wink your eye, tilt your head, wave good-bye. Then, go on girl, put on your show.

THE END

Mirror, Mirror on the wall!
Who is the most beautiful girl of all?
What sets me apart from the rest?
I'll share with you what makes ME the best!
I am SMART. I am BEAUTIFUL. I am ENOUGH.

Complete the following sentences to identify your positive qualities.

I am GREAT at _____

I feel HAPPY when _____

I am most PROUD of _____

I feel BEAUTIFUL when _____

I am FABULOUS because _____

My family LIKES it when _____

The following activities can be used individually or in small groups.

For individual use, encourage your special young lady to answer the following questions.

1. Name one thing you are good at doing.
2. What makes you feel happy?
3. Tell me about a time you were proud of yourself.
4. When do you feel beautiful?
5. Share two positive qualities your friends like about you.

For individual and small groups

1. **"I Am" Collage** - The girls bring in a picture of themselves and glue it in the middle of a poster board or construction paper. Encourage girls to cut-out pictures or words from magazines that describe their personality and glue them around their picture. Allow the opportunity to share with the group.

2. **Name Acronyms** - Have girls write their first name vertically on construction paper. Next to each letter, write down positive words that begin with the same letter and describe their good qualities. Allow them to decorate with things that make them happy.
   Example: K - Kind
   A - Athletic
   Y - Young
   L - Likeable
   A - Awesome

3. **"You're Fabulous Because…"** - In a group setting, have girls write their name on a slip of paper or index card, place them in a bowl and mix them up. Without looking, have each girl select a name from the bowl. For younger girls: Have girls sit in a circle and take turns saying something positive about the girl sitting next to them.

   For older girls: Have them write down one thing that makes their chosen girl fabulous. Another option for older girls: Have girls write down positive qualities about each other. Collect and sort them. Then, hand the papers or cards out to the named individual. Each girl will have multiple positive messages about why they are fabulous.

   Example: " _____ , you are fabulous because you _____ . "

4. **Positive Affirmations** - Encourage girls to write down positive affirmations to place in visible locations they can see everyday (bedroom, notebook, locker, etc) as a reminder of their positive characteristics.

   Example: "I am smart. I am beautiful. I am enough."

ABOUT THE AUTHOR

Candace Petty Smith, is an elementary school counselor who loves to encourage and empower children to be their best. She is also the author of *Someday...*, a story of a young boy with dreams of becoming a professional athlete. Candace plans to continue creating stories that provide motivation and confidence in children and will also serve as a resource for parents and educators.

Follow Candace:

Email: candace@candacepsmith.com

Web: candacepsmith.com

 candacepsmithauthor

 candacepsmithbooks

cpsmithauthor

Made in the USA
Middletown, DE
09 August 2021